I'M A MINGER!

Alex Jones

I'M A MINGER!

OBERON BOOKS
LONDON

First published in 2008 by Oberon Books Ltd
521 Caledonian Road, London N7 9RH
Tel: 020 7607 3637 / Fax: 020 7607 3629
e-mail: info@oberonbooks.com
www.oberonbooks.com

Reprinted 2010

A catalogue record for this book is available from the British
Library.

ISBN: 978-1-84002-873-7

Cover design by Nettie Edwards (Lumilyon)

Printed in Great Britain by Antony Rowe Ltd, Chippenham.

For Lucy

Characters

KATIE plays all of the following –

TORI

SOPHIE

WANKER WILLIAMS

PATRICK PEASBODY

OLIVER BUNTING

DAD

ROGER BOSTOCK

MELANIE FOSTER

SAM

MUM

VERITY EDWARDS

HEATHER PLEBY

TREENA SHARPLES

LUCY CUNNINGHAM

MR CUNNINGHAM

KELLY PARKER

LAMB

RACHEL HAMPSHIRE

INTERNET VOICES

ROB

RINA

LIN

I'm a Minger! was first performed at the Arts Theatre, Great Newport Street, London, on 14 July 2008.

The play was subsequently performed in a revised version at Theatre 503 on 25 August 2008 with the following cast:

KATIE, Alex Jones

Director Amy Bonsall
Designer Maira Vazeou

This published text is the one performed at Theatre 503. If a school or youth theatre wants to perform the play with a large cast, it might be worth reinstating the text cut for this production, which has been included as an Appendix (pages 53–78).

SCENE 1

A teenage girl's bedroom: posters of boy bands and various pin-ups of hunky men, together with pictures of cute animals – cats and horses, etc. It's pink and girly, but it's a real mess: make-up, hair slides, magazines, books, videos, CDs, clothes, empty cups, plates, cushions and cuddly toys are everywhere. This is a room that is so untidy it's reached a point of no return: this is KATIE's bedroom, her refuge and her prison. Music – 'Teenage Dirtbag' by Wheatus as KATIE, a 14-year-old girl, flounces through the door, dressed in her school uniform. She angrily throws her schoolbag on her bed. Music ends.

KATIE: I don't believe it! *Cow!* Bloody cow – I hate her,
    I really, really hate her! Cow! Bitch! Cow, cow, cow!!
    (*Shouts.*) *Aagghhrr!!*

KATIE calms down, and then –

Bitch!!

KATIE is suddenly aware of the audience and decides to confide in them.

(*To audience.*) Kelly, right, Kelly the bitch decides to have a party on the very same night of my sleep-over – the very same night! And I know she's done it on purpose, and she invites everybody, doesn't she? Sophie, Tori, Heather, Sam – even Treena…except me of course.

Deflated, KATIE goes over to the mirror and looks at her reflection.

Hello fatty!

She leans in closer and examines her face.

Oh my God – look at my skin. Even my spots have got spots. Was I born ugly, or did I just evolve into ugliness?

KATIE leaves the mirror and sits dejected on her bed.

I was looking forward to it: a sleep-over at my house. I said to Tori 'You're still coming, aren't you?' And she said –

She becomes TORI and whenever another character crops up she becomes that one too.

TORI: Um…well, you see Katie, Kelly's like had a hard time lately; she's had a hard time. Her dog died, didn't it?

KATIE: *Her dog?* So what? It's a dog; it's an animal, what's the big deal?' (*To audience.*) And Sophie says –

SOPHIE: She loved that dog, actually. She cried for two days solid, she did.

KATIE: When? When did she cry? I never saw her cry.

SOPHIE: That's because she does it in private, okay? She keeps it to herself, but deep down inside she's bleeding, she is.

KATIE: (*To audience.*) And I'm thinking *Really? How nice – hope she bleeds to death then.* But I say 'But Sophie, we arranged the sleep-over weeks ago.'

SOPHIE: That's typical of you, Katie – always think of yourself. That's really selfish.

KATIE: No I'm not selfish; I was just looking forward to having you around, that's all. Dad was gonna buy us all pizzas and we could rent a DVD and do our make-up and stuff, that's all. I mean, yeah if Kelly needs you…well maybe we could do it the following Friday? (*To audience.*) And Sophie says –

SOPHIE: Yeah – maybe.

KATIE: And Tori goes –

TORI: I'm busy that weekend, Pat an' Simone's coming over.

KATIE: I don't know why I bother; I might as well face up to the fact that I'm unpopular and when I leave school I'll become a nun or a lesbian, or both probably knowing me. And then we had RE, didn't we with slimy Mr Wanker Williams, and I hadn't done my homework, had I?

WILLIAMS: T, t, t! No homework again. Well what a surprise.

KATIE: But sir, I did it, but I did it in rough in my notebook and I was gonna hand it in tomorrow when I copied it up, honestly sir.

WILLIAMS: And some fell upon stony ground.

KATIE: (*Smart.*) No sir, it's not on the ground, it's at home.

WILLIAMS: Don't be insolent with me, Katie Weller; I won't have it, I simply won't have it, do you hear?

KATIE: But sir…

WILLIAMS: (*Loud.*) *Do you hear me?!*

KATIE: (*Submissive.*) Yes sir.

WILLIAMS: Detention after school on Thursday – don't forget to inform your parents that you'll be late home.

KATIE: But sir, I'll miss the school bus.

WILLIAMS: Not my problem. Sort out an alternative mode of transport, or take the bipedal route.

KATIE: What?

WILLIAMS: Your legs. Walk girl – walk!

KATIE: *Wanker!*

KATIE calls down the stairs.

Dad!

Pause.

Dad!!

Pause.

Deaf old bat. (*Screams.*) *DAD!!!*

DAD: No need to shout.

KATIE: Really?

DAD: What do you want, Katie?

KATIE: What's for dinner?

DAD: (*Proudly.*) Spag Bol.

KATIE: (*To herself.*) *Oh God!* (*To her DAD.*) Can I have something else?

DAD: No, you're eating spaghetti bolognese…and tidy your room!

KATIE looks in the mirror and sticks out her chest.

'Least I've got tits. (*Smiles.*) Kelly's got a chest like a fat boy. *Jealous cow!* Patrick Peasbody was looking at them today – I saw him. I said 'What you looking at?' and he went all red –

PATRICK: Nothin' Katie, honestly.

KATIE: And Oliver Bunting said –

OLIVER: He was lookin' at yer tits, Katie, weren' he? An' I don't blame him, either – they're fantastic!

KATIE: And I blushed a bit and felt really proud… *Spag Bol* – I hate Spag Bol; it's like eating…it's like eating shit. It *is* shit, actually, that's what it is – minced up shit with garlic and basil. *Basil?* Who wants leaves in food?

DAD: It's classic Mediterranean cookery, Katie.

KATIE: Am I supposed to be impressed, Dad?

DAD: What about that fish we ate last night?

KATIE: It had a head!

DAD: Grilled Red Snapper.

KATIE: It had a head, Dad!

DAD: It had been marinaded.

KATIE: Yeah, but why?

DAD: Because…well…

KATIE: See, what's the point?

DAD: It took me ages to make that marinade: three teaspoons of arrowroot, lemon grass (outer leaves removed, finely sliced), fresh ginger…

KATIE: I hate ginger – all ginger should be banned; especially hair; I'd cross the road rather than talk to a ginger-headed person.

DAD: The juice and zest of one lime…

KATIE: Apart from Roger Bostock, he's all right.

DAD: Two tablespoons of Thai fish sauce…

KATIE: He catches my bus sometimes; he spoke to me last week.

ROGER: Hi Katie.

KATIE: (*Flustered.*) Oh yeah…hi, erm…

ROGER: Roger?

KATIE: Oh yeah, Roger, I knew that; I mean I really did, Roger, I really did, I mean I don't want you to think I don't know your name because I do…it's erm, it's Roger.

ROGER: I know.

KATIE: (*Laughs*) Yeah, of course you do; I mean of course you do, it'd be daft if you didn't, so of course you do.

ROGER: So – how's things?

KATIE: Well…you know –

ROGER: No, that's why I'm asking.

KATIE: Yeah, 'course, yeah. Well they're okay, actually, yeah things are like…okay.

ROGER: Still doing the ballet?

KATIE: *No!* Bloody hell, no! You must be joking! Who told you that?

ROGER: Nobody. I just wondered that's all. I mean, I know you used to do it; I saw you in that show last year at the Hall; I thought you looked great.

KATIE: Did you?

ROGER: Yeah, thought you looked great...in your tutu. (*Laughs.*)

KATIE: Huh, yeah my tutu. (*Embarrassed laugh.*)

ROGER: *Swan Lake*, wasn't it?

KATIE: It was, yeah

ROGER: I love ballet.

KATIE: You like ballet?!

ROGER: I know it's strange for a boy to like ballet, but who gives a toss what anybody thinks, eh?

KATIE: (*To audience.*) *Who gives a toss? Who gives a toss?* I couldn't believe my ears – such bravery! Ohh, I love the way the light shines in his eyes – they're sort of green and his freckles...well they're kind of not so bad when you get used to them. (*Back to ROGER.*) Yeah, I know what you mean, who gives a toss?

ROGER: Still, shame you don't do it anymore; I thought you were pretty good at it.

KATIE: Oh I am... I mean, I'm not saying I'm good at it, because well that would like be bragging, wouldn't it? But what I meant was I am still doing it – ballet, I mean.

ROGER: But you just said you weren't.

KATIE: Did I?

ROGER: (*Smiles.*) Yeah.

KATIE: Oh… I wonder why I said that?

ROGER: I don't know.

KATIE: Well… I think I said it because…because…

ROGER: It's not cool?

KATIE: Er…

ROGER: Don't let your peers put pressure on you and stop you being creative – I don't, no way; I still play in the local youth orchestra.

KATIE: Do you? Oh Great. I saw you play once, actually.

ROGER: Did you?

KATIE: Yeah, saw you playing your trumpet.

ROGER: Violin.

KATIE: Trumpet, violin – similar really.

ROGER: (*Laughs.*) Yeah, 'cept one's Brass and the other's Strings.

KATIE: (*Laughs.*) Yeah, that's what I meant. (*To audience.*) My God, do I sound as thick as I think I sound?

ROGER: Well Katie, reckon you an' me've got to keep the flag of culture flying, don't you?

KATIE: Definitely, definitely!

ROGER: 'Cause if we listen to our peers…

KATIE: (*To audience.*) I love the way he says that – *'Our peers',* it sounds so…so… I dunno sort of intellectual an'…well sexy, actually. I could never sound intelligent – oh, I get sick of all those dumb blonde jokes, not that I don't like being blonde 'cause I do, instead of having to dye it every three weeks like Melanie Foster – you should see the way her roots show through – they look minging, really minging.

MEL: Can you see my roots, can you see them, Katie?

KATIE: No, not at all.

MEL: 'Cause I want you to tell me if you can.

KATIE: No, I can't Mel, honestly.

MEL: 'Cause you know what – I think I look more blonde than you, yer know?

KATIE: (*To audience.*) In your dreams, you chavvy, pikey, wannabe blondie loser! Huh, more blonde than me – I am one hundred and sixty one per cent nat-u-ral, baby, and you'd better believe it, you jealous mousy-haired cow!

ROGER: 'Cause if we listen to our peers…

KATIE: (*Sighs.*) *Peers!*

ROGER: We're just going to hold ourselves back; creatively I mean.

KATIE: (*To ROGER.*) I agree totally, Roger, I really do, one hundred per cent; I dunno why we bother listening to them.

ROGER: So let me know when you're in your next show and I'll come and see you.

KATIE: Will you?

ROGER: I'd love to see you in your tutu again.

KATIE: Would you?

ROGER: (*Smiles.*) Yeah.

KATIE: And I'd love to see you in your trumpet, I mean violin; I mean see you play it, not in it. (*Embarrassed laugh.*)

ROGER: (*Laughs.*) You're cool.

KATIE: (*To audience.*) He said that, he really did, and he's in year eleven, too…!

DAD: Fifteen grammes of fresh coriander, roughly chopped…

KATIE: (*To DAD.*) Are you still here?

DAD: And all served with an aubergine and pesto salad!

KATIE: *It had a head!*

DAD: All fish have heads.

KATIE: Only in the sea – how am I supposed to eat something that's looking at me?! (*To audience.*) Still I can get rid of it later; just chuck it up an' flush it away. It was Tori who taught me to do that, actually, at Sam's birthday sleep-over at primary: we'd stuffed ourselves stupid; so we were in the bathroom and she just threw up in the toilet. '*Euurggr!*'

TORI: What's the problem?

KATIE: You just threw up!

TORI: So?

KATIE: But Tori, you just threw up!

TORI: Yeah – can't you?

KATIE: Well…yeah if I have to.

TORI: Katie, you are such a retard!

KATIE: No I'm not. (*To audience.*) And Sam chimes in –

SAM: Yes you are Katie. We can all chuck up at will; we've been doin' it for ages.

KATIE: Have you?

SAM: Do you wanna get fat?

KATIE: No.

SAM: (*Mimicking.*) '*No*'. Oh, show her Tori –

KATIE: And she did.

DAD: Aubergine and pesto salad – when do you get to eat that?

17

KATIE: (*To DAD.*) Never again, hopefully: fish is not supposed to be served with salad, Dad – it's unnatural; it goes against all the laws of nature.

DAD: I try to cook you nice food; a little appreciation would not go amiss.

KATIE: But Dad, I don't like nice food; I like proper food.

DAD: Oh just…just…*tidy your room!*

KATIE: (*To audience.*) Tidy my room? Why? It's my room, it's not his, it's not Mum's – it's mine!

KATIE picks up a fluffy toy, helplessly looking for somewhere to put it.

(*Sighs.*) Where am I supposed to put everything? It's a bedroom, not a bloody Tardis! *Fuck – fuck, fuck, fuck, fuck, fuck, fuck, fuck!!* That's better! Know what? Melanie Foster swears all the time – in front of her Mum, too. I was round her house, 'cause well I was walking home with her, wasn't I? 'Cause we'd both been in detention together, I mean I wouldn't normally hang out with her because she's…well she's a chav and she's scary, too.

MEL: Wanna come in; watch some telly?

KATIE: Erm…

MEL: Watch MTV if yer like. We got Sky – you got Sky?

KATIE: No.

MEL: You ain't got Sky?!

KATIE: No, we ain't… I mean we haven't.

MEL: God, you're deprived, you are.

KATIE: Tell me about it.

MEL: Get all the footy an' all. You watch the footy?

KATIE: No, not really.

MEL: You don't watch the footy! You are deprived, girl; really deprived!

KATIE: (*To audience.*) Anyway, just as I'm giving up the will to live, we're by her house in Skylark Rise, which is like a really scary area where all the chavs and pikeys live and all the gardens are full of nicked cars and rusty motorbikes and old baby buggies an' stuff, and before I know it I'm in there.

MEL: (*Shouts.*) Mum!!

KATIE: And her mum shouts back from up the stairs –

MUM: *What?!*

MEL: Any tea?

MUM: I dunno, do I? See what's in the fridge!

MEL: I've got me mate wiv me!

MUM: So?!

MEL: So you gonna fuckin' cook us summat?

MUM: Leave off, Mel; I've got a minging hangover!

MEL: Arse'ole!

MUM: Whatever!

MEL: Fuck her! Let's rustle summat up, eh? You like fuckin' burgers?

KATIE: Yeah.

MEL: Chips?

KATIE: Yeah, yeah I do.

MEL: Got some microwave ones – eat 'em straight from the fuckin' box; they're fuckin' great!

KATIE: (*To audience.*) So we sat on her greasy real leather sofa together in her living room with bright orange carpet and racing pictures on the wall, and we watched MTV on the biggest telly I have ever seen, and we ate burgers, beans microwave chips, jaffa cakes and coke from a tray on our laps – *it was fucking great!*

KATIE's phone bleeps.

Text message – wonder if it's Sophie?

KATIE retrieves the message.

(*Reading*) *A girl was granted two wishes by a genie. She asked for bigger tits and a tight cunt...* (*Laughs.*) that is disgusting...! Oh there's some more... (*Scrolling down.*) *So the genie gave her a pair of 38 double Ds and your mobile number...* Huh... funny...who sent that? (*Scrolls down*) Number withheld... I'm not tight; nobody could call me tight, nobody; I even gave Sophie my Monster Munch last Thursday; pickled onion flavour too – so nobody can call me tight, nobody!

Pause.

Maybe I should text Sophie? But if it was her an' she got a text from me, she'd know that I knew she'd sent it... Still I could text her anyway, just text her 'cause she's a mate... (*Begins to text.*) *Hey Sophe, wot u doing? Not homework I hope...*er...what else can I say...? *Shit for dinner 2 night, or should I say spag bol – eughhhrr!! Txt back – ur Monster Munch Mate... LOL.* Shall I send it..? Oh, I'll send it, just send it 'cause she's a mate – have a laugh. (*Presses send.*) I wish I hadn't sent it! Oh God, it looks a bit desperate; like I'm desperately trying to be desperate and crave her friendship.

MUM: (*Calls.*) *Hello!*

KATIE: (*To audience.*) *Uhh*, that'll be Mum.

MUM: (*Calls.*) Katie! Katie! I'm home!

KATIE: (*To herself.*) Yeah, yeah, I can hear you.

MUM: Katie, are you going to come and give your Mum a hug?

KATIE: (*To audience.*) A hug? A bloody hug! She doesn't deserve one.

MUM: I've been at work all day, teaching.

KATIE: (*To herself.*) Then don't bloody teach.

MUM: And I come home to a stroppy daughter who can't even be bothered to acknowledge a mother who works all hours to put a decent meal on the table.

KATIE: (*To audience.*) Grilled snapper – a decent meal?

MUM: And buy you new outfits from Top Shop and H&M almost every weekend!

KATIE: (*To audience.*) That is blackmail, that is! That is emotional blackmail!

MUM: Right, sod you! Just don't expect me to fork out for that skirt you saw last week or those shoes either for that matter.

KATIE leaps up and mimes running down the stairs to hug her MUM.

KATIE: Mum! Mum, is that you? Sorry, I had my Ipod on.

MUM: I bet! Anyway, had a good day? What did you do at school?

KATIE: Stuff.

MUM: What stuff?

KATIE: Just stuff, Mum.

MUM: What sort of stuff?

KATIE: I dunno – stuff; the same stuff we do everyday – I don't know what else to say – *stuff!*

MUM: (*Bemused.*) All right, only trying to take an interest in what you do.

KATIE: *Huh!*

MUM: And what's that supposed to mean?

KATIE: Oh come on Mum, to be fair, when do you ever show an interest in what I do?

MUM: I'm always interested in what you do.

KATIE: *Huh!*

MUM: Stop saying *huh*! Have you got any homework?

Pause.

Have you got any homework?

KATIE: (*Quiet.*) A bit, but it doesn't have to be in till next week.

MUM: Go and do your homework; don't leave it until the last moment again.

KATIE: (*About to strop off.*) *Mum* – you've got to buy me that new outfit this weekend.

MUM: Got to?

KATIE: I've got to have it for the school disco.

MUM: You've got plenty of nice clothes already.

KATIE: *You must be joking!* I haven't got anything, absolutely anything! You can't do this to me, Mum, you can't! You promised me you'd buy me that skirt from Top Shop, you said you would, you promised! And those shoes…and I need a new top, too.

MUM: Look Katie, I'm sorry, but I've got lesson plans to do this weekend.

KATIE: But the disco's next Friday. Sam and Sophie and Tori and absolutely everybody in the school, actually are all like having new stuff… I thought it would be nice to go out together, have a little Mummy and daughter time.

MUM: Oh…you know all the right buttons to press to make me feel guilty.

KATIE: (*Pouting.*) Please?

MUM: (*Sighs.*) I'll pick you up from school on Monday.

KATIE: Thanks Mum – I love you! (*To audience.*) *Sucker!*

MUM: Now go and get on with your homework; dinner won't be long.

KATIE: (*Ironic, to audience.*) Oh – *how lovely!* Still, I can just chuck it up later an' stuff my face with chocolate to take the taste away. See what you're doing to me, father, you selfish, bloody cordon-blue freak – *You're making me fat!* God – I hate my fucking life!

KATIE's phone beeps; she looks alarmed as she picks it up.

Text – shit, it's from Sophie – oh God…what is it?

She scrolls down.

'Hi Monster Munch Buddy. I am staring at a blank page that something should be written on is wot I am doing! Fuck homework. Wot U wearing 2 disco? LOL – Sophe.' (*Beams.*) Aw, she called me her Monster Munch Buddy! Aw, what a mate – I love Sophe I do! Right – I've got to get those fuckin' shoes! See ya –

Music - 'Dontcha!' by Pussycat Dolls as KATIE bounds out. Lights fade to black.

SCENE 2

Lights up. Music continues from last scene as KATIE enters with carrier bags, delighted with her purchases. Her room is still the same as before – a complete mess.

KATIE: *Shopping! Shopping, shopping, shopping!* I love it! Wait till you see what I've got –

She pulls out a very short skirt from an H&M bag.

Look at that – it's like just what I wanted, exactly and like it's really, really short and I don't think Mum realised just how short it was and I wouldn't let her see me in it because I know what she'd say…

MUM: You are not going out in a skirt like that; your Dad would have a fit.

KATIE: But Mum, it's not that short.

MUM: Katie, I can see your knickers!

KATIE: No you can't, anyway it's just how everybody wears them now.

MUM: It's obscene, I am not buying you that skirt.

KATIE: (*To audience.*) But she did, because I came out of the changing room and said, 'It fits, Mum, can I have it?'

MUM: Why didn't you let me see you in it?

KATIE: Come on, Mum; people are like queueing up for the changing rooms two deep.

MUM: It seems a bit short.

KATIE: Not when it's on.

MUM: Really?

KATIE: Really Mum, I wouldn't wear anything too short anyway; I don't want to look like a tart. Can I have it, or not?

MUM: Oh all right.

KATIE: (*Beams.*) Thanks Mum! (*To audience.*) And then we went into New Look and they had these well cool shoes…

KATIE takes the shoes from the box, discarding packaging anywhere.

MUM: Are you sure you can walk in them okay?

KATIE: Yeah, they're really comfortable, actually. (*To audience.*) They're fucking instruments of torture, but who gives a shit – they look amazing!

KATIE drops the shoes and pounces on another bag.

Oh, and wait till you see my top; correction – two tops! I got Mum to buy me two, 'cause they were only a fiver each, well one was a fiver; the other was a bit more expensive.

MUM: Twenty quid for a top, that's a bit steep.

KATIE: But Mum, the other one was only a fiver; you can't count that as a purchase really.

MUM: What? How did you work that one out?

KATIE: (*Holding it in front of her.*) Oh but Mum, look at it; it's really sweet. I'll never see another one like this, ever, and it's not as if I get that much, really.

MUM: I took you shopping a couple of months ago.

KATIE: Exactly Mum, months, not weeks – *months!* Like styles change from day to day. (*To audience.*) Anyway, I worked my dutiful daughter routine on her and she coughed up. (*Suddenly.*) Guess what? I saw Roger Bostock again on the bus and he came right over and sat by me, and like I go red instantly, but it's like wow, he likes me, he really does! And he says…

ROGER: Wotcha Kate.

KATIE: (*To audience.*) And I try to stop blushing, but I can't and I hope he doesn't notice and I say back… 'Wotcha Roger; how's the trumpet?'

ROGER: Violin.

KATIE: Oh yeah, violin, I keep getting them mixed up; I don't know why 'cause one is like wind and the other is like… er…er…

ROGER: Strings?

KATIE: Yeah – strings (*Laughs*).

ROGER: (*Smiles.*) You're funny.

KATIE: Oh…thank you, I mean if like that's a good thing I mean.

ROGER: Yeah, it's good. Saw the ballet tickets were on sale. Looking forward to seeing you in your tutu.

KATIE: (*Laughs.*) Wow, you're really coming then?

ROGER: Got the tickets.

KATIE: Already?

ROGER: Like I said, bit of culture; don't get much around here.

KATIE: It's only my dance school, though; it's not like The Royal Ballet or anything.

ROGER: Hey, it doesn't matter, just be good to see some dance – especially as you're in it.

KATIE: (*To audience.*) He fancies me; I mean he must, mustn't he…but like, why doesn't he just ask me out? Perhaps he just likes me as a friend? Oh God, I'm so confused and I've got to rehearse more now; I haven't been to class for over a week! Oh God! And Sophie saw us talking, didn't she and she had to come over then of course.

SOPHIE: Hi, what you two talking about then?

KATIE: (*To audience.*) And I'm thinking; don't mention the show, please don't mention the show!

ROGER: I'm going to see Katie's ballet show, actually.

SOPHIE: My God Katie, I thought you'd given all that stuff up!

KATIE: (*To audience.*) And I could see that she was like eyeing up Roger. Anyway, Roger right, Roger was totally unfazed by all this and he just smiles at Sophie and says…

ROGER: I take it dance is not your cup of tea then?

KATIE: (*To audience.*) And Sophie is really on the spot now and a bit stuck for words.

SOPHIE: No… I… I didn't mean that I don't like dance, 'cause like I really love dancing, you know proper dancing, like at a club or something… (*Smiles.*) Anyway if you like dance so much, you should come out with us sometime, go to Tramps; bit of lippy, bit of make-up I can charm the bouncers and get us in, you fancy a bit of a night out, Rog?

KATIE: (*To audience.*) I couldn't believe it! Sophie – Sophie, my best mate stealing the love of my life away from me. But I didn't have to worry, 'cause Roger just looked at her as if she was some sort of uber chav, and said…

ROGER: *Dancing…at Tramps nightclub…? Lippy, make-up..? Charm the bouncers…?* Don't think so, not my cup of tea.

KATIE: (*To audience.*) So right, at lunchtime I was on my own 'cause Sam and the others were off on the geography trip and Sophie went off bumming that posh girl from year eleven, and she was only doing it to get back at me 'cause of what happened with Roger Bostock…

SOPHIE: He's such a dork!

KATIE: Come on, Sophe – he's like a film star, or something and he's in year eleven.

SOPHIE: He's got ginger hair!

KATIE: Yeah, nothin' I can do about that.

SOPHIE: And what's with the ballet thing? Is he like gay, or something? Oh my God, I bet he's gay, I bet he is!

KATIE: There is no way he is gay, no way and you know it… (*To audience.*) My God, he can't be, can he? I mean he does sort of have a strange obsession with tutus; yeah, but it's because he wants to see me in one, that's all. I don't mind wearing a tutu for him…bit weird, though. Anyway, Sophie was being all huffy with me and so I was on my ownsome and feeling a bit vulnerable, and I saw Rachel Hampshire with Verity Edwards and her posse, and so although they're not cool or anything I went over, and they were all really nice actually and we had quite a laugh, and we were talking about the end of term disco and Verity said…

VERITY: You can come over to my house and get ready with us if you like, Katie.

KATIE: (*To audience.*) *Isn't that nice?* But there is no way I could, or even would 'cause they're like the loser group really, and after a while I could see that Sophie was on her own, having been cold-shouldered no doubt by posh girl. God, she is like so bloody moody at the moment… 'You due on or summat?'

SOPHIE: No I am not! And what's that supposed to mean?

KATIE: Oh come on Sophe, chill out, let's go to tuck shop an' I'll buy you some Monster Munch, eh? (*Suddenly to audience.*) You know what? They've banned crisps in tuck! Why pick on crisps? I fuckin' hate Jamie Oliver! I will dance on his grave when he dies, Kelly Parker's too! And Heather Pleby who used to be a really good mate until she started hanging out with Treena Sharples, who is such a wannabe everything: bitch, slut, goth, troubled teenager, etcetera, etcetera. And so now Heather pretends that she doesn't know me and if I say hello, she goes…

HEATHER: *What?*

KATIE: (*To audience.*) And…

HEATHER: Hello…whoever you are.

KATIE: (*To audience.*) And right she has put on so much weight she looks like Shrek, and her school skirt is so tight round her fat arse that it's split up either side, and the buttons are bursting on her shirt, which I swear is see-through, and rolls of fat bulging under her massive fucking grey bra that she never changes.

KATIE surveys her room, despondent.

Dad's still going on about my room…

DAD: It's disgusting. You can hardly open the bloody door!

KATIE: But Dad, it's 'cause I've got so much homework; I can't do both. I've got RE homework, right, which is like a totally random essay about what would you do if you were God? (*To audience.*) Actually I know exactly what I'd do if I was God; I would turn Roger Bostock's hair blonde, marry him and have lots of sex… I haven't actually had sex yet, but I'm pretty sure I'd like it because I once snogged my cousin's mate who is a year older than me and he put his hand inside my bra and it was great! (*Suddenly.*) You know what? Heather Pleby, right, she's always going on about sex like she's done it, but she hasn't and she can't anyway because she's too fat; she's even fatter than Kelly Parker if that's possible!

HEATHER: You talkin' 'bout me?

KATIE: No.

HEATHER: Why you lookin' at me, then?

KATIE: I wasn't.

HEATHER: Well make sure you don't.

KATIE: (*To audience.*) And she's always backed up by her scabby side-kick, Treena goth-face slut…

TREENA: Yeah you were, you was lookin' at her, like in like a funny way, me too, you were.

KATIE: (*To audience.*) Yeah, well maybe it's because it's not often you get to see the Elephant Woman and Mrs Dracula in one place.

TREENA: I think you was looking at my scars, that's what I think.

HEATHER: Was you looking at her scars?

KATIE: What scars? (*To audience.*) And then the dork of a fuckin' Emo rolls up her sleeve to show me where she cuts herself…

TREENA: Those right – those scars!

KATIE: *Eughhrr!*

HEATHER: What do you mean – *eughhrr?* You saying her scars are ugly?

TREENA: Yeah, you saying I make you feel sick, or summat?

KATIE: No, not at all; I'm not saying that Treena, I wouldn't; it was just like an instant reaction.

HEATHER: Why do you think she does it, eh?

KATIE: Er…

HEATHER: Why?

KATIE: Is it like…a fashion statement?

HEATHER: She does it because of people like you, you fucking cow!

KATIE: (*To audience.*) And then the pair of them march off like the bloody Gestapo to terrorise some other poor, unsuspecting kid. School is just full of weirdos like that; there's hardly anybody normal… (*Suddenly.*) So…where was I? Oh yeah, (*To DAD.*) so right Dad – I've got RE homework and maths and…

DAD: I don't care how much homework you have young lady; I still expect you to keep your room tidy.

KATIE: (*To audience.*) I hate it when he says that – young lady – Old Man! You try tidying it; it's just not that easy – it's like…where does it all come from? But no, I have to miraculously tidy it all away like I'm Mary fucking Poppins!

KATIE picks up some clothes – they're totally scrunched.

Uhh – should be ironed, really…uhhh –

KATIE looks around for somewhere to put it, but is instantly distracted by her shopping and holds up her new skirt.

Look at that – I am gonna look so cool at the disco. I've invited the girls around here again to get ready. They all came last year; it was great. And we're all swigging cider an' swappin' lippy an' doing each others hair an' listenin' to music, and then we all crowd into Dad's car and hit the disco…which wasn't that great to be honest – well who was there to get off with – Oliver Bunting?

OLIVER: Your tits look nice, girls!

KATIE: (*To audience.*) *Eughhr!* Or Patrick Peasbody…

PATRICK: (*Awkward laugh.*) 'Lo Katie, you look… (*Awkward laugh.*)

KATIE: What? What do I look, Patrick?

PATRICK: Y' know… (*Awkward laugh.*) you look…

KATIE: *What?* (*To audience.*) And Oliver Bunting, who is his vocal partner, says…

OLIVER: He thinks yer look sexy an' he wants to shag yer!

PATRICK: No I don't!

OLIVER: Liar!

PATRICK: No…

OLIVER: Well if you won't, I will.

PATRICK: Well… I suppose…

KATIE: (*To audience.*) And like, do they seriously think I'd let either of them pop my cherry? The grubby, dirty little losers…and Treena Sharples was pissed in the toilet all night trying to slash her wrists with a piece of wire, while Heather Pleby banged on the door and slagged off everyone that came near. She scared poor Verity Edwards shitless…

VERITY: Is she all right, Heather?

HEATHER: No she is not all fucking right, you nosy little cunt!

VERITY: Oh…anything I can do?

HEATHER: Yeah – *die*.

VERITY: Well… I'd better get back to the disco I suppose.

HEATHER: Yeah, turn your back on human suffering like everybody else in this fucking school…bitch! (*Shouts.*) Hang on in there, Treen – I love yer, mate, you can count on me.

TREENA: (*Crying.*) Life is so fuckin' horrible, Heather!

HEATHER: Yeah I know, Treen, I know.

KATIE: (*To audience.*) That's school discos for you! (*Suddenly glum.*) Had another text today…sort of joke thing again: *'How do blonde brain cells die…? Alone'.* (*Sadly.*) And I weighed myself today and I've put on two more pounds, and my hips are just bloody massive. And of course Lucy Cunningham just had to say something, didn't she?

LUCY: Hhm, bit of a spare tyre coming there, Katie; I'd watch that if I were you.

KATIE: Cheeky cow! Just because she's got weight issues. She is *well* anorexic; I mean the proper thing – she looks like a stick insect and she's always going on about being size zero, the bitch..! (*Sighs.*) And then the next day she'll go…

LUCY: Oh look at me – I'm so fat!

KATIE: Just so everyone will go, 'No you're not, Lucy, you're really thin, you're size zero, wish I could be size zero'. And she struts around school like this –

KATIE minces around pathetically on her toes.

She looks like she's disabled; she walks on tiptoe and she like talks in this stupid whingy-whiney voice all the time…

LUCY: Oh I wish I wasn't so fat, I really do.

KATIE: *Aahhh* – I want to strangle her, I really do! Or just pick her up and snap her in half over my knee like the dry, brittle piece of balsa wood that she is!

KATIE's phone beeps a message. She grabs it.

A message! (*Grins.*) I am so popular! (*Suddenly wary.*) What if it's another slaggy text though? Oh God, I can't bear it; why is someone doing it to me?

She scrolls down.

(*Reading text.*) *'How's your pirouettes coming on?'* What's that supposed to fucking mean? *'Can't wait to see you do the Dying Swan!'* What..? *'LOL – Rog…'* (*Delighted.*) My God, it's from him! It's from him! It's from Roger from year eleven with a brain like a computer and a beautiful smile and freckles and a fit body and he's a boy and he's texted me! Right – fuck homework and tidying my room – where's me tutu? I need to practise! See ya!

Music – 'My Humps' by Black Eyed Peas. Lights fade to black.

SCENE 3

Music – 'Dance of the Sugar Plum Fairy' by Tchaikovsky. KATIE dances into her bedroom wearing a tutu and performs the Sugar Plum Fairy. The music reaches its conclusion – she curtsies to the audience.

KATIE: What do you think? I'm still a bit wobbly on the développé stuff, but Miss said I was really coming on and wondered if I hadn't considered a career in dance? *Me?*

Fucking hell, I don't think so…! God, I'd have to lose weight then though 'cause dancers are all like really thin and I think you have to smoke too… Hope old ginger-nut appreciates all this effort. We sat together on the bus again last Friday, and you know what – he gave me a book. And right it's by Charles bloody Dickens! And get this right, inside he's writ'…

ROGER: Gotta get a bit of culture, Katie!

KATIE: Cheeky bastard! I'm cultured, I've got loads of culture I have… So anyway I *have* started to read it 'cause you never know he might just say…

ROGER: How you getting on with it then, Katie?

KATIE: (*To audience.*) And then I'd have to lie and say 'Um yeah, it's great, really exciting stuff, Rog'. (*To audience.*) And then he might just say…

ROGER: So where you up to?

KATIE: Oh right, yeah you know, the bit where it's all…like… Victorian.

ROGER: Victorian?

KATIE: Yeah, you know with like everyone having to eat gruel all the time and even coal… (*To audience.*) They did eat coal, didn't they? Or was that the Elizabethans…? No… I don't think you *can* eat coal… But then like a few hours has gone by and I'm still reading, and now I'm thinking what a tosser that Mr Murdstone is – (*Suddenly.*) and what a nasty evil thing to do to make poor little David Copperfield wear a sign at school that said *Take care – this boy bites*. God, you'd never get away with that now; but if you could I'd stick one on Kelly Parker saying *Take care – this girl bitches!* Yeah, (*Enjoying it.*) yeah and one on Oliver Bunting saying *This boy is a sex pervert!* And one on Melanie Foster saying *This girl is not naturally blonde.* Talking about hair, he caught me staring at him, actually… I couldn't help it because

I was trying to imagine what it must be like to wake up every morning with hair that colour; and he said...

ROGER: You're looking at my hair, aren't you?

KATIE: (*To audience.*) And I went all hot and red and felt really guilty and embarrassed... 'No...not really, erm... I mean... I'm sorry, I didn't mean to... I mean (*Heartfelt.*) oh, it must be horrible for you!'

ROGER: Horrible?

KATIE: Well...don't you ever wish you didn't have ginger hair?

ROGER: No way, why would I?

KATIE: Well... I dunno... I mean it's like...it's...

ROGER: Ginger?

KATIE: (*Nods, sadly.*) Yeah.

ROGER: Well I don't get it about ginger hair and all the prejudice about it; it's so random and pointless, I mean it's just hair – what's the problem? Not only that; it's one of the most unique hair colours in the world – it's the rarest.

KATIE: Is it?

ROGER: Yeah, it's a recessive gene; bit like blonde hair, really. Don't you wish you weren't blonde?

KATIE: No way – I love it! Apart from the dumb blonde jokes of course.

ROGER: There you go – ginger, blonde; they'll always find something to trash someone with; just so long as it's not them. But the truth is Katie; anyone who can be bothered to take the piss out of someone's hair is frankly lacking intelligence, or is socially inept.

KATIE: (*To audience.*) *Socially inept!* Where does he find such phrases – he is so fucking cool! And you know what? His hair is like so...well sexy to be honest – it kind of reflects the light in a really pretty way, and I swear it sort of sparkles a bit too. I dunno why I was so prejudiced about ginger hair; ginger hair is actually now my favouritest hair colour in the world…after blonde of course. (*Suddenly.*) *Why doesn't he ask me out?!*

KATIE looks at herself in the mirror, pinches her waist.

Gotta lose some weight before the concert; I look gross! Wonder what culinary feast Dad's cooking up tonight?

KATIE calls down the stairs.

KATIE: (*Shouts.*) Dad, what's for dinner?!

No reply. She calls again.

(*Shouts.*) Hey deafo, what you cooking?!

DAD: (*Proudly.*) Moroccan lamb with couscous.

KATIE: (*Sighs.*) Uhh…can I just have some salad?

DAD: It's Moroccan lamb with couscous.

KATIE: Well can I just have some salad?

DAD: It's delicious – you'll love it.

KATIE: *Daad*, please don't make me eat it?

DAD: It's a classic Mediterranean dish, you're very lucky to be served such food. And have you tidied your room yet?

Pause.

Have you tidied your room?

KATIE: I've been practising my ballet, all right?!

DAD: Well now practise tidying your room, young lady. And don't come down till you've finished.

KATIE: (*To audience.*) That is so unfair! It's like whatever I say, it's always *Tidy your room, young lady!* Bloody food fanatic, feeding me poor little Moroccan baa lambs.

KATIE picks up a fluffy toy lamb from her bed.

LAMB: *Baa, baa;* please don't eat me, Katie! I'm only three days old – I don't want to end up being sicked up in the toilet.

KATIE: I'm sorry lambykins, I really am, but what choice do I have? He's a mad food fanatic.

LAMB: *Baa, baa!* Well I just hope he appreciates the fact that my pure innocent lamby blood has been spilt for his culinary obsession...

KATIE: (*Suddenly, glum.*) Sophie's took me off her top ten on her My Space... I don't get it; I'm really hurt... I mean – why? And I knew I shouldn't have, but I asked her, didn't I?

SOPHIE: Have I?

KATIE: Yeah, you have, Sophe, 'cause I was online last night an' you know I couldn't help noticing and well it sort of hurt me a bit... (*To audience.*) And Tori and Sam were there and you could just tell that they knew all about it, and Sam said...

SAM: God, Katie it's like just a list, that's all; it's just a list.

KATIE: Yeah I know, but just think how you'd feel, Sam. (*To audience.*) And then Sophie sneers and goes...

SOPHIE: I don't know what it is with you lately, Katie, but like everyone is just getting a little bit pissed off with you.

KATIE: Everyone – who?

SOPHIE: *Everyone.*

KATIE: Well what exactly have I done to piss everyone off?

SOPHIE: It's just...it's just your attitude, okay?

KATIE: (*To audience.*) And I couldn't say anything else, 'cause I was getting all choked up and had to go to the toilets and cry. And then I had another text, didn't I: *'What does a blonde and a beer bottle have in common? They're both empty from the neck up...!'* I bet it's Kelly Parker – she's on Sophie's top ten list, cow! God I hate her so bloody much: her clip-on hair extensions are crap – like fake Barbie hair! And her face is so round and she puts foundation on her lips so they're the same colour as her face; which I just can't deal with – why does everyone like the fugly slut so much!! (*Calms down.*) Anyway, disco's this week; something to look forward to; and the girls are all coming round here again.

MUM: (*Calls.*) Katie!

KATIE: (*To audience.*) Oh God... (*To MUM.*) *I'm tidying it, all right!*

MUM: I just wanted to have a chat. Your Dad's noticed you've not been yourself lately; he's worried about you. You look a bit...want to talk?

KATIE: I'm okay.

MUM: Sure?

KATIE: Yeah.

MUM: Look, I know I always seem to be busy, but I'm here for you if you need me; we both are, okay?

KATIE: Okay Mum.

MUM: Love you.

KATIE: You too.

MUM: (*Smiles.*) Your room's a bit of a mess.

KATIE: *I know!* (*To audience.*) God, why do they have to make me feel so guilty? And all I do is vomit up his poxy Mediterranean dinners... Know what? I can't actually eat anything anymore without having to go to the toilet and throw it up afterwards...and like I'm always feeling tired and bloated and I dunno, why can't I just be like...*normal?*

KATIE's phone beeps a message.

Text from Sophie – *'Girls and me won't be able 2 cum round ur house tomorrow. CU by tennis courts at 8.' What?* What's all that about? It was arranged – we were all going to get ready here and Dad was gonna drop us off again like last time – it was arranged. What is it with me? Why am I such a fucking stupid fat stupid loser! *And I can't tidy my room, I can't! I just fucking can't!*

Collapses on her bed, crying. Music – 'Complicated' by Avril Livigne. Lights fade to black.

SCENE 4

Lights up. Music continues from last scene. KATIE enters wearing her disco outfit, staggering on her high heels. She sits on the bed and throws her shoes across the room.

KATIE: (*Weepy.*) It was just horrible! It was; I mean I don't know where to start – it was horrible! Like when I got to school I saw them all in a huddle by the tuck shop with Kelly pug-face Parker, and l thought, don't make a big thing about the text, but I had to say something... 'So, can't make my house this year – why's that?' (*To audience.*) And Sophie goes...

SOPHIE: Yeah, sorry 'bout that, but you know; my Aunt's coming over with her new baby.

KATIE: What about you lot? You can still come, can't you? (*To audience.*) And Tori's like...

TORI: Know what, Katie; it's just too much hassle, like getting over there after school; it's quicker just to get ready at home, know what I mean?

KATIE: So we're all meeting up at eight by the tennis courts, right?

SOPHIE: Yeah – eight.

KATIE: You sure, Sophe, 'cause I don't wanna be standing on my own like some sad loser.

SOPHIE: I said yeah, I said eight, so we'll be there at eight.

KATIE: (*To audience.*) And everybody was like edgy and different and Sophie was being well bitchy.

SOPHIE: God Katie, what is your problem? We said we'd be there at eight – what is your problem?

KATIE: I haven't got a problem; just wanna make sure, that's all. (*To audience.*) And then Tori chips in as well…

TORI: We told you though, Katie, we told you and you just keep going on about it; it's like really boring.

KATIE: Sorry, sorry for being so boring! (*To audience.*) Then Sam has a go too…

SAM: Fucking hell, Katie, like give it a rest, yeah? You're like so *'poor me!'* all the time.

KATIE: I'm not. I'm just a bit upset, I guess.

SAM: *Whatever!*

KATIE: I mean, I thought we were all gonna get ready together like we did last year. (*To audience.*) And then Sam gave Tori a look as if to say, *'Don't say anything.'* So I knew they were meeting up, probably at fat Kelly's house! And oh my God, listen to this, this is really terrible – Lucy Cunningham hasn't been at school for ages, and today in assembly, right, her Mum and Dad were there on stage; and Mr Broden the head said that they wanted to have a word with us all about their daughter, Lucy because they felt what had happened to her could happen to any of us, and we knew instantly that it was about her anorexia and it went all quiet, and Mrs Cunningham couldn't speak because she was crying so much, but Mr Cunningham patted her hand and oh, it was so sad – he stood up in front of the whole school, and you could tell that he was fighting back the tears…

MR C: You may have noticed that Lucy hasn't been at school for a while…she is in fact in hospital, and is very seriously ill… She's an anorexic and has starved herself so much that her internal organs have literally stopped working…we may in fact lose her…and she's our daughter and we love her and we can't bear to think of a life without her around… My wife and I felt we wanted to come here today to say to anyone who has any such problems; please don't keep them to yourselves, don't leave it until it's too late… speak to someone, seek help, because you're all so young and have the rest of your life in front of you, and…and…

KATIE: (*To audience.*) And then he started crying too, *really crying*, and it was awful to see how upset they were, and afterwards, right, in the corridor, right after assembly, Kelly says…

KELLY: Hope she fucking dies, the fucking freak!

KATIE: (*To audience.*) And all the girls laughed – and I couldn't believe it, so I said… 'Actually I don't think that's funny, Kelly – imagine if it was you'… And my God did I say the wrong thing…

KELLY: You saying I'm fat, Katie?

KATIE: No, not at all – I was talking about Lucy Cunningham. (*To audience.*) And then Sam goes…

SAM: Yes you were, that's what you were insinuating.

KATIE: No, no I wasn't! (*To audience.*) And then Kelly is like in floods of tears and runs off to the toilets and Sophie turns round and says…

SOPHIE: You bitch, Katie, you fucking bitch! You know how sensitive she is about her weight!

KATIE: (*To audience.*) So then I had to get ready all on my own and Dad dropped me off at eight and I waited nearly an hour before I went inside and there they were… 'I've been standing by the tennis courts for nearly an hour!'

SAM: Didn't Sophe text you?

KATIE: No Sam, she didn't!

SAM: Oh, right well she must have forgot; we decided to meet inside 'cause it's so cold.

KATIE: Yes – I know; I was freezing my tits off out there!

SAM: All right, calm down!

KATIE: (*To audience.*) And I just knew they'd done it on purpose, and I felt so awkward, because they were all whispering and nudging each other and I knew they were slagging me off and then Kelly said…

KELLY: Where'd you get that skirt from then, Katie?

KATIE: (*To audience.*) And I couldn't believe that that fugly ho-bag slut would even dare to criticise my dress sense when she looked like King fucking Kong in her skinny leggings with a disgusting camel toe and muffin top cellulite dripping out. But no, the fat tart really did have the audacity to say…

KELLY: Bit short… I thought you didn't like your legs.

KATIE: (*To audience.*) That started the rest off, Sam…

SAM: And what's with the shoes?

KATIE: They cost a fortune, actually. (*To audience.*) Sophie…

SOPHIE: Pity you can't take them back then.

KATIE: (*To audience.*) Tori…

TORI: A kilt – that is so last year, Katie.

KATIE: (*To audience.*) Kelly again…

KELLY: A sparkly top with a kilt, what are you thinking?

KATIE: (*To audience.*) And believe it or not, even Treena Sharples…

TREENA: You *minger!*

KATIE: And that was that, from then on all night long, every couple of minutes somebody would say *Hiya minger!* or *You look minging!* or just *Minger!* And before the night was out I even started to get texts – *Hello minger, You minger!* etcetera, etcetera… So I was on my own in the corridor and Verity Edwards was coming back from the toilets, and it was obvious I'd been crying, and she came over…

VERITY: Hey Katie, you okay?

KATIE: (*Weepy.*) Um, yeah, yeah, I mean…you know…it's just…

VERITY: Sophie?

KATIE: Yeah – it's…well it's Sophie and Tori and Sam and and…and…

VERITY: Kelly Parker?

KATIE: How did you guess?

VERITY: Yeah, she can be a right bitch!

KATIE: *Tell me about it!* (*To audience.*) So we chatted for a while and slagged off a few bitches and bullies, and I began to feel a bit better, and then Rachel came over too, and she was really nice as well…

RACHEL: Hello Katie, looking forward to your ballet show.

KATIE: *You're coming to see it?*

RACHEL: I saw you last year too. She was great, Vez – you should have seen her.

KATIE: (*Proudly to audience.*) And then the rest of their posse came over and it was really nice, 'cause they were talking about me and about how good I was at ballet…but then Kelly and the others came round the corner and I could see they were laughing and I just choked up again and rang Dad to come and pick me up, and he could see I was upset, and all the way home he just kept on…

DAD: You okay?

KATIE: Yeah.

…ju seem upset, has someone upset you?

KATIE: No.

DAD: So why are you leaving early?

KATIE: Just tired.

DAD: Come on sweetheart, you can tell me, what's up, eh?

KATIE: (*Snaps.*) Nothing Dad, just leave it, right!

DAD: Okay…but if you want to talk about anything, anything at all, just remember I'm here.

KATIE: God, you don't fucking stop, do you?!

DAD: Hey, all right, there's no need for language, young lady, however you feel.

KATIE: *Well just get off my back then!* (*To audience.*) And the texts just kept coming – *Minger, minger, minger!* So there you are – I'm a minger! And I was so upset and there was no one to call and talk to, so I just went on line and I don't know why, but I googled *suicide*…and I clicked on this chat line site…

KATIE is at her computer.

And there were all these kids talking about it…

Loads of different voices of kids; boys and girls from different parts of the country…

VOICES: They keep calling me fat… I just want to die… You're the only friends I've got… I *am* fat… And there's no one to talk to; I feel so lonely… I cut myself again – I'm covered in scars… So what – wear longs sleeves… Been nicking my mum's anti-depressants, got quite a collection… I'm so, so fat – I hate myself… Do it man – just do it!

KATIE: (*To audience.*) And before I know it I'm typing (*KATIE taps at the keyboard.*) 'My name is Katie and I'm a minger' (*To audience.*) And straight away, someone called Rob types back 'Welcome to the site, Katie; we're all mingers here'

(*To audience.*) And I had to laugh at that, so I began to chat with everyone, and it was like at last here's someone who understands, who really understands my pain, and I told them about Kelly and the others and how depressed I was, and someone called Rina said...

RINA: You ever thought about killing yourself?

KATIE: (*To audience.*) And it sent like a shock through my body 'cause you know what – suddenly it like seemed possible that I could; just give up on everything, make all my problems disappear and wouldn't they fucking remember me then, the bastards! But then I thought about Roger and the ballet show next week; something good to look forward to, because I think he's gonna ask me out very soon, and like who needs friends then...? He is so hot, and I just know he's going to rescue me from my woes and my pity and my mingerishness. Oh God, please ask me out you ginger twat! *Please, please, please!*

Music – 'I'll Put A Spell On You' by Aqualung.

Lights fade to black.

SCENE 5

Music as KATIE enters her room (which is still a complete mess), dressed in her school uniform. She throws her bag on the bed and sits, dejected.

KATIE: Another shit day! On my own again – the sad loser minger kid with no one to hang out with! They are such horrible fucking bitches... I wish they'd be my friends again... And Mum and Dad are still nagging me about my room...

DAD: Tell you what, if it's not tidy by the end of the week – no pocket money!

KATIE: Please yourself.

DAD: I'm not joking.

KATIE: I don't fucking care – all right?!

DAD: Don't you speak to me like that! I will not have that kind of language in this house!

KATIE: Oh… *fuck off!*

DAD: Right get up to your room, young lady and no telly – I mean it!

KATIE: *Fine*! (*To audience.*) He came…he came to the show; I saw him in the audience…with a girl. I peeped through the curtains before it started. I think he was just stringing me along for a joke, and then just rubbing my face in it with his bloody girlfriend! (*Tearful, angry.*) How could I have been so stupid – why would someone like him fancy an ugly fat cow like me! So then I had to go out there and dance my little heart out for the son-of-a-bitch ginger cunt's warped sense of humour. On the way out, he even had the fucking gall to hang around, grinning and taking the piss…

ROGER: Hey Katie – you were great!

KATIE: Really?

ROGER: Yeah – loved your tutu!

KATIE: Know what Roger? I'll buy you a fucking tutu for your birthday, you weirdo! (*To audience.*) He looked shocked, so I thought maybe I've got it wrong, so I went back inside, but the two of them were just like all huddled up with their arms around each other; haven't spoken to him since; he's even stopped catching the bus – he cycles to school – how could he, I mean why? Why would you just want to hurt someone like that, I don't get it… Lucy Cunningham's dead…she died yesterday and all of a sudden everybody in the school is claiming her as a friend, and like there's flowers all round the school gates and everyone is crying and hugging each other and saying what a great girl she was and so full of life – fucking hypocrites! Even I used to slag her off…behind her back though…she's dead – 14 years old and she's dead – what's that about? Know what?

This is really gonna make you laugh; know what – I've been cutting myself – straight up, no kidding; everyone does it on the site, they talk about it all the time…

VOICES: Should see my arms – a mass of scars… I cut my legs too… I do it when I get in from school, best time, no one at home… I love the buzz – it's the best… I know someone hit an artery, blood all up the walls…that's dumb, just cut into the skin.

KATIE: So I thought I'd see for myself, so I got one of Dad's chef's knives from the kitchen and I pressed it against my arm and straight away I'm bleeding, and this is the weird thing right – I could see why Treena and all those Emos do it; 'cause it was like a release, like the pain was dripping out of me and now I'm like doing it all the time.

MUM: Katie! What is going on with you?

KATIE: Nothing.

MUM: Really, well I had a call today from your school – it seems you haven't handed in any homework for weeks and that you're openly rude and aggressive to your teachers. What on earth is going on?

KATIE: Nothing.

MUM: Katie, I'm really worried – this is your education you're messing up.

KATIE: (*Shrugs.*) Don't care.

MUM: Really, well how do you think that makes me feel? I am working so hard at the moment, and who do you think I do it for?

KATIE: Who?

MUM: You! You; so that you can have new clothes and nice holidays and I dunno…whatever you want.

KATIE: Yeah, well don't bother if it's such an effort. You can't buy love, Mum.

MUM: Thank you, thank you very much. And why did you swear at your Dad just now?

KATIE: Felt like it.

MUM: I am so disappointed in you, so very, disappointed… *tidy your room!*

KATIE: Mum… Mum… I… (*To audience.*) Oh God I feel so guilty… I don't deserve such nice parents, I don't…and they deserve better than me…all I ever do is moan and complain and… I can't tidy my room, I just can't!

KATIE throws stuff around the room; kicks cuddly toys, completely losing it.

I can't do it!! I can't!! I give up! I just give up!!

She collapses on her bed, distraught, and then she pulls herself together, goes to the computer, logs on and begins typing.

Hi – Katie here. Just wanted let you all know that I'm going to do it right now…

VOICES: Go for it Katie – you are so brave… Sometimes it's the only thing to do… See you on the other side… I love you, Katie – you are an inspiration…

KATIE: I love you guys too, you're the only real friends I've ever had.

VOICES: Make it painless, Katie – don't suffer… No more suffering…

KATIE: Got some paracetamol, should do the trick. Bye… (*To audience.*) I'm going to have so many friends tomorrow, just like Lucy Cunningham.

She goes to her bedside table and takes out loads of packets of paracetamol, sits on her bed and begins to empty them on her duvet. She stuffs some in her mouth and curls up beneath the duvet. Music – 'How To Save A Life' by The Fray. Lights fade to black.

SCENE 6

Music continues. Lights up. KATIE is sitting on her bed dressed in her school uniform.

KATIE: No, you are not in heaven and I am not an angel; I'm still here and you're still going to have to put up with my effervescent charm and my witty witticisms a little while more, I'm afraid. Dad came up for a chat 'cause he was worried and he found me…and well it wasn't very nice for him. So – *they made me sick.* Don't ever want to go through that again, I can tell you – gross or what? A couple of nights in the hospital and then a few days in bed, just talking. I told Mum everything…

KATIE: I'm so scared, Mum.

MUM: I know baby, I know.

KATIE: My friends, my eating…all this cutting myself.

MUM: And I've been so wrapped up with my work I didn't even notice.

KATIE: And I can't tidy my room on my own; I can't Mum – it's impossible! (*To audience.*) And so she helped me, right – right there and then, and she found a place for everything and vacuumed the carpet and dusted an' stuff, and it was great to have a tidy room again; it really was… Yeah, well it *was* last week! And then Dad came in…

DAD: Know what – who fancies some fish and chips?

KATIE: (*To audience.*) And I looked a bit suspicious…

DAD: The proper kind without a head on and lots of crispy batter.

KATIE: From the chip shop, Dad?

DAD: Good idea – from the chip shop!

KATIE: *Yeah!* (*To audience.*) Then I had to get back to school and face the bitches. Dad got me a new SIM card, so I don't have to worry about those stupid texts anymore. And anyway, got myself a whole bunch of new mates now and they're coming round for a sleepover this Friday – Verity, Rachel, Charlotte and Lin; Lin is so funny; she does this impression of Wanker Williams that is like spot on…

LIN: (*Impression.*) If you cannot get a bus from school, take the bipedal route – and who called me a wanker?

KATIE: (*Laughs.*) That is brilliant, Lin, brilliant! (*To audience.*) See – Vez saw me sticking my fingers up at Sophie, 'cause she called me *minger* again and she said…

VERITY: Yeah, it's about time you dumped Sophie and that lot!

KATIE: (*To audience.*) And I was just about to say *I didn't dump them, they dumped me,* when I thought *no, actually – let everyone think it was the other way round…* 'Yeah, they are like so self-obsessed.'

VERITY: Yeah, an' that Kelly; shallow or what – *fat cow!*

KATIE: (*To audience.*) And I thought…*what a nice girl!* And so we started hanging out and like they are just *nice girls*; they're not bitchy at all, well not *that* bitchy, 'cause you've got to bitch a bit. (*Smiles.*) Right are you ready for this? I have actually got a boyfriend – *I have!* And I bet you can't guess his name – it's Roger Bostock! Oh, I can't believe it, I just can't, he is like so wonderful! He's just…*ohhh!* He's gorgeous and kind and lovely and sexy and bloody hell can he kiss; I mean wow! And I felt so stupid – it was his cousin he was with, and he was really upset because he thought I didn't like him and was just playing a game… 'That's what I thought you were doing.'

ROGER: No way, Katie, no way. Why would I ever do something as shallow as that?

KATIE: (*To audience.*) He just appeared again one day on the bus… 'Thought you didn't catch the bus anymore.'

ROGER: Well that's because of you; I mean I don't understand why you did that.

KATIE: Did what exactly?

ROGER: Said that stuff to me at your concert; I thought you liked me.

KATIE: I thought you liked me!

ROGER: I did… I mean *I do*.

KATIE: I saw you with that girl.

ROGER: What girl?

KATIE: She had her arms around you, Roger; she was hugging you.

ROGER: Because I was upset. Oh, hang on, you thought… she's Annabelle, my cousin; she loves ballet, so I brought her along. So then I thought you didn't like me and you were just playing a game.

KATIE: That's what I thought you were doing.

ROGER: No way, Katie, no way. Why would I ever do something as shallow as that?

KATIE: (*To audience.*) So we've been an item ever since, and like you should see how jealous Kelly and that lot are. In fact Kelly actually said to me the other day…

KELLY: Don't know how you can go out with someone with such ginger hair, Katie, I really don't.

KATIE: Actually Kelly, ginger hair is the most unique and rarest hair colour in the world (next to blonde), because it's a recessive gene.

KELLY: And what exactly is a *recessive gene*?

KATIE: It's…well it's like a gift from God.

KELLY: Well maybe my hair is a gift from God too!

KATIE: No Kelly, you don't get clip-on hair extensions from God, you get them from that cheap accessory stall in the market! (*To audience.*) And I see them sometimes strutting about the place like they're so cool, but they're not; they're just pathetic and bitchy, and there's always one of them crying because one of them has said something to upset the other, and I wonder why I ever bothered to try and fit it with the twisted logic of their stale and vacuous lifestyles – by the way I'm using more words and phrases like that these days, like it – *got to get a bit of culture!* But now, I've just got one last thing to say to you lot –

KATIE stands on her bed and sings along to 'Hello Sunshine' by Super Furry Animals, from the verse beginning 'I'm a Minger.' She curtsies, blows kisses to the audience and exits.

THE END

Appendix

TEXT CUT FROM THE THEATRE 503 PRODUCTION

FROM SCENE 1, PAGE 10…

SOPHIE: That's typical of you, Katie – always think of yourself. That's really selfish.

KATIE: (*To audience.*) And I'm going red and my heart's beating fast and I can feel my eyes welling up, but I choke it back: 'No I'm not selfish; I was just looking forward to having you around, that's all. Dad was gonna buy us all pizzas and we could rent a DVD and do our make-up and stuff, that's all. I mean, yeah if Kelly needs to see you…well maybe we could do it the following Friday?' And Sophie says –

SOPHIE: Yeah – maybe.

KATIE: And Tori says –

TORI: I'm busy that week end, Pat an' Simone's coming over.

KATIE: And one-by-one they all drop out and I see my sleep-over slowly disintegrate before my very eyes. I don't know why I bother; I might as well face up to the fact that I'm unpopular and when I leave school I'll become a nun or a lesbian, or both probably knowing me.

KATIE scrambles about under her bed and pulls out a shoe box, which she opens and takes out a chocolate bar.

KATIE: You're my friend, aren't you?

KATIE makes the CHOCOLATE BAR talk.

CHOC: Yes of course I am. But I'll make you fat and ugly and spotty if you eat me.

KATIE tears the wrapper off.

KATIE: Shut up!

KATIE takes a bite and instantly feels guilty.

Oh God, I'm gonna regret that. It's Kelly's fault – bitch! And then we had RE, didn't we with slimy Mr Wanker Williams, and I hadn't done my homework, had I?

FROM SCENE 1, PAGE 11…

DAD: No need to shout.

KATIE: Really?

DAD: What do you want, Katie?

KATIE: What's for dinner?

DAD: (*Proudly.*) Spag Bol.

KATIE: (*To herself.*) Oh God! (*To her DAD.*) Can I have something else?

DAD: I'm sick of cooking separate meals – you'll have the same as us.

KATE: Well can I just have some pasta with cheese, then?

DAD: No, you're having Spaghetti Bolognese…and tidy your room!

KATIE slams the door shut.

KATIE: Spag Bol – great!

KATIE wearily surveys the tip that is her room.

How can I tidy this? There's nowhere to put it all. Don't they understand? Doesn't anyone understand?

KATIE picks up the CHOCOLATE BAR.

CHOC: I understand, Katie.

KATIE: Shut up! You just want me to get spots!

KATIE looks in the mirror and sticks out her chest.

'Least I've got tits. (*Smiles.*) Kelly's got a chest like a fat boy. Jealous cow! Patrick Peasbody was looking at them today – I saw him. I said 'What you looking at?' and he went all red.

FROM SCENE 1, PAGE 15…

KATIE: (*To audience.*) I love the way he says that – 'Our peers', it sounds so…so… I dunno sort of intellectual an'…well sexy, actually; and he speaks like that all the time! It'd take me a million years to be able to sound intelligent, it really would – oh, I get sick of all those dumb blonde jokes, not that I don't like being blonde 'cause I do, and I know that Sophie an' Tori an' Sam an' well any girl without blonde hair, actually would give their right arm to have natural blonde hair instead of having to dye it every three weeks like Melanie Foster with her bloody plate-thick base an' pencilled-in lip-gloss – you should see the way her roots show through – they look minging, really minging.

FROM SCENE 1, PAGE 16...

ROGER: (*Laughs.*) You're cool.

KATIE: (*To audience.*) He said that, he really did, and he's in year eleven, too! Nobody, and I mean nobody apart from him has actually said that to me and I believed them...

DAD: Fifteen grammes of fresh coriander, roughly chopped...

KATIE: Are you still here?

DAD: And all served with an aubergine and pesto salad!

KATIE: It had a head!

DAD: All fish have heads.

KATIE: Only in the sea – how am I supposed to eat something that's looking at me?!

KATIE picks up a soft toy and makes it become the fish.

FISH: How could you eat me, Katie? How could you eat me?

KATIE: I'm sorry fish, but I have to; my Dad makes me.

FISH: What a cruel man!

KATIE: You have no idea, fish, no idea.

FISH: I only want to swim around the ocean talking to my friends the shrimps and the dolphins; I don't want a clove of garlic shoved up my arse and three small chillies (finely chopped) rubbed into my beautiful silver scales!

KATIE: I'm right there with you, fish; but what can I do? I'm trapped in this hell-hole and have to eat whatever is put before me; including Red-bloody-Snapper with its head on... Still I can get rid of it later; just chuck it up an' flush it away. It was Tori who taught me to do that, actually, at Sam's birthday sleep-over at primary: we'd stuffed ourselves stupid; so we were in the bathroom and she just threw up in the toilet. 'Euurggr!'

FROM SCENE 1, PAGE 20…

KATIE: Text message – wonder if it's Sophie?

KATIE retrieves the message.

(*Reading.*) *A girl was granted two wishes by a genie. She asked for bigger tits and a tight cunt…* (*Laughs.*)… Oh there's some more… (*Scrolling down.*) *So the genie gave her a pair of 38 double D's and your mobile number…* Huh… funny…who sent that? (*Scrolls down.*) Number withheld… just a joke…it's only a joke, that's all; quite funny really – 38 double D's and a tight cunt (*Laughs.*)… I'm not tight; nobody could say I was tight, nobody. Bet it was bloody Kelly, bet it bloody was, bloody cow…! Nobody could call me tight; I even gave Sophie my Monster Munch last Thursday when we went on that trip to that bloody boring bloody museum of really old boring stuff that's supposed to be historic and really interesting, but is in fact just old and boring and everything inside it should just be thrown in a skip or burnt on a big bonfire made of science books. Anyway there we were having a break, sitting on the steps outside, and I got my lunch out and Sophie said…

SOPHIE: Oh God, Monster Munch, I love Monster Munch – what flavour are they?

KATIE: Pickled onion.

SOPHIE: Oh no, don't, not pickled onion – only my favourite of the favouritest Monster Munch there is in the world – and I've got to watch you eat them?

KATIE: Do you want one?

SOPHIE: Aw, one isn't enough with Monster Munch though is it?

KATIE: (*To audience.*) And Kelly, right, fat-faced, bloody Kelly with a packed lunch that would feed a whole country, Kelly goes…

KELLY: I'll have one, Katie.

KATIE: (*To audience.*) And I thought you scrounging little scrubber. So I said to Sophie… 'Do you want them?'

SOPHIE: What? You'd give me your Monster Munch – the whole packet, pickled onion flavour, too?

KATIE: Yeah, you can have them if you like. (*To audience.*) Anything rather than let Kelly get her grubby little mitts on them.

SOPHIE: Aw, that's a real mate that is, that's a real mate who would give her Monster Munch to her hungry, deprived friend…you sure?

KATIE: Go for it, not that hungry, actually.

SOPHIE: Aw, thanks Katie, I love you I do. What a lovely thing to do, what a mate.

KATIE: (*To audience.*) And I was feeling all sort of warm and glowing and proud in my benevolence, and then Kelly goes…

KELLY: Can I have one, Sophe?

SOPHIE: Sure, get stuck in.

KATIE: (*To audience.*) Stuck in? She ate half the bloody packet, and I had to stand there and watch the puffy-faced, flabby bitch stuff her face with my Monster Munch, which I actually like more than crisps, actually, and I couldn't have one even though they were mine because I'd said I wasn't that hungry. So nobody can call me tight, nobody!

Pause.

Anyway, it was just a joke I reckon, not about me really. It's about this girl and the genie… Sophie wouldn't send that, nor Sam or Tori. Bet it was Kelly, fat bitch…tight? Not me mate, not after the great Monster Munch benevolence, no way… Maybe I should text Sophie? I mean if it was her an' she got a text from me, she'd know that I knew she'd sent it… She wouldn't though; she wouldn't send something like that to me – her Monster Munch Mate…! Still I could text her anyway, just text her 'cause she's a mate… A mate that's going to Kelly's party though… I'm gonna text her… (*Begins to text.*) *Hey Sophe, wot u doing? Not homework I hope…er…what else can I say…? Shit for dinner 2 night, or should I say spag bol – eughhhrr!! Txt back – ur Monster*

59

Munch Mate… LOL. Shall I send it..? Oh, what if it was from her? No, couldn't be, she wouldn't. Shall I send it? She probably thinks I'm bumming her 'cause she's going to Kelly's party. Oh, I'll send it, just send it 'cause she's a mate – have a laugh. Yeah – I'll send it. (*Presses send.*) I wish I hadn't sent it! Oh God, it looks a bit desperate; like I'm desperately trying to be desperate and crave her friendship. And what if she had sent that joke; she'll just think I'm being all creepy and weird, texting back like I'm some kind of weirdy weirdo…oh bloody shit! Why did I send it? Nah, it'll be all right; she'll text back in a minute, sure too…yeah…yeah, be all right. God, stop being paranoid… Come on, come on – text back. Come on, Sophie – it's me, Katie your Monster Munch mate… She's probably turned her phone off – no, she never turns her phone off; nobody turns their phones off. (*Suddenly.*) *Oh my God!* What if me and Roger Bostock had children and they had ginger hair! I wouldn't mind having red hair; it's just that horrible ginger colour. What am I gonna do? How can I marry him and bear his ginger children? *Eughhr* – can you imagine pushing a baby buggy and Tori or Sophie or somebody came over and said *'Oh, let's have a look at your baby…' and it's ginger! No, no, nooo!!*

KATIE picks up her mobile again.

Is there a signal? Sometimes can't get a signal up here? Yeah, got a signal…wonder if she got it…wonder if she likes me? Yeah, 'cause she does, 'specially after the great Monster Munch benevolence.

A door slams off.

That'll be Mum.

MUM: (*Calls.*) Hello!

KATIE: (*To audience.*) I can't have his children, not if they have ginger hair, no way.

MUM: (*Calls.*) Katie!

KATIE: (*To audience.*) Wonder if you can get like some kind of treatment to stop them being ginger? Like genetic engineering or something?

MUM: (*Calls.*) Katie! Katie! I'm home!

KATIE: (*To audience.*) Better go and be the dutiful daughter, I suppose.

MUM: (*Calls.*) I'm home darling!

KATIE: (*To audience.*) Not that she's ever the dutiful mother.

MUM: (*Calls.*) I'm home!

KATIE: (*To herself.*) Yeah, yeah, I can hear you.

FROM SCENE 1, PAGE 22…

KATIE: Oh come on Mum, to be fair, when do you ever show an interest in what I do?

MUM: I'm always interested in what you do.

KATIE: Huh!

MUM: Stop saying huh!

KATIE: God, you're moody tonight.

MUM: I have a right to be moody after a day spent with a class of obnoxious eight year olds.

KATIE: (*Changing the subject.*) Mum – Dad's cooking Spag Bol, can I just have some pasta and cheese?

MUM: Your Dad enjoys cooking for us; you could at least show some appreciation.

KATIE: It's got garlic and basil and all sorts of foreign rubbish in it. And why can't we have pasta shapes? Spaghetti is just too complicated!

MUM: Have you got any homework?

FROM SCENE 2, PAGE 27…

KATIE: (*To audience.*) I couldn't believe it! Sophie – Sophie, my best mate stealing the love of my life away from me; how could she do it? And why – why if she's like such a good friend and all. But I didn't have to worry, 'cause Roger just looked at her as if she was some sort of uber chav, and said…

ROGER: *Dancing…at Tramps nightclub…? Lippy, make-up…? Charm the bouncers…? Don't think so, not my cup of tea.*

KATIE: (*To audience.*) And Sophie was red with fury and embarrassment and said…

SOPHIE: Well…yeah if you ever change your mind…

KATIE: (*To audience.*) And sauntered off to bum the posh year eleven girl, but someone else had taken her place, so she had to sit next to Verity Edwards.

VERITY: (*Sweetly.*) Hello Sophie.

SOPHIE: *Huh!*

VERITY: Looking forward to the disco?

SOPHIE: Whatever!

KATIE: (*To audience.*) Hey, guess what I did today? Only scored a round in rounders I did; like me who is like totally crap at games and anything to do with sports or running or jumping or catching a ball, or anything remotely physical at all. Anyway, we were playing rounders and Tori who is like really sporty was just getting all worked up because I was in her team and we were losing; and like who gives a fuck, it's fucking rounders, it's a bloody stupid game where you hit a ball with a bat that's not even a proper bat 'cause it's round and like a tube, but she's going…

TORI: *Come on Katie, hit the ball, just hit it, that's all you have to do, hit it!*

KATIE: (*To audience.*) And I'm thinking '*Shut the fuck up, you sport-obsessed fitness freak!*' and I keep missing the fucking ball.

TORI: *Hit the ball, Katie! Hit it – it's not that difficult!* God, why did I have to have you on my team?

KATIE: And then right it's my last go at hitting it before I'm out and all I can hear is Tori wailing away in my ear when Sam throws the ball at me and in my anger and frustration I lean back and *whack* – I hit the ball and it's like sailing away across the chain-link and I stand there looking at it, sort of not believing it, and then I hear Tori shouting…

TORI: *Run, run you dork!*

KATIE: So I run all round the whole of the posts and everyone is cheering me – *me*! Good stuff, or what? But right, at lunchtime I was on my own 'cause Sam and the others were off on the geography trip and Sophie went off bumming that posh girl, Lindsey Davison from year eleven, who had friends of her own, and you could see that she was just like irritating her, and she was only doing it to get back at me 'cause of what happened with Roger Bostock…

FROM SCENE 2, PAGE 28…

SOPHIE: No I am not! And what's that supposed to mean?

KATIE: Nothing. Oh come on Sophe, chill out, let's go to tuck shop an' I'll buy you some Monster Munch, eh? (*Suddenly to audience.*) You know what? They've stopped selling crisps in tuck! I love crisps; I mean I really love them, like I'd marry them if I could, that's how much I like them. Why pick on crisps? They never hurt anybody; all they ever did was bring pleasure to people in their little sliced potato way. But wait, get this – they still sell donuts! What is that all about? And they charge you eighty pence for something that tastes like a piece of bloody bog roll dipped in grease! And they ban crisps, which actually when I come to think of it are vegetables – they are, they're bloody potatoes, and potatoes unless I'm very much mistaken are in fact a very popular member of the vegetable community, and so they are in actual fact good for you! So what's that all about, eh? What's all that about? And while we're about it – I can't remember the last time I saw a chip in the canteen. I fuckin' hate Jamie Oliver! I will dance on his grave when he dies, Kelly Parker's too! And Heather Pleby who used to be really nice, but then she started hanging around with Treena Sharples, who is such a wannabe everything: bitch, slut, goth, troubled teenager, etcetera, etcetera, and she's pathetic because they're all pathetic things to want to be. And so now Heather pretends that she doesn't know me and if I say hello, she just goes…

HEATHER: *What?*

KATIE: (*To audience.*) And…

HEATHER: Hello…whoever you are.

KATIE: (*To audience.*) And I think how can you pretend not to know me when you used to come round my house and I'd do her hair an' stuff. But now she pretends she doesn't know me; now that she's a slut an' all and she looks like Shrek…and right she has put on so much weight that her school skirt is so tight round her fat arse that it's split up either side, and the buttons are bursting on her shirt, which I swear is see-through, and rolls of fat bulging under her massive fucking grey bra that she never changes. She's so big she looks like a…a building, like a bungalow in fact, no a house, no come to think of it – a block of flats; and I wish a plane would just come and crash into her like that tower thing in America!

KATIE surveys her room, despondent.

Dad's still going on about my room…

DAD: It's disgusting. You can hardly open the bloody door!

KATIE: But Dad…

DAD: And it's starting to smell. You don't even bring your coffee cups down, or your cereal bowls…or anything!

KATIE: But Dad…

DAD: *What?*

KATIE: But Dad, it's 'cause I've got so much homework; I can't do both.

DAD: Why not?

KATIE: It's physically impossible, it really is. I've got RE homework, right, which is like a totally random essay about what would you do if you were God? (*To audience.*) Actually I know exactly what I'd do if I was God; I'd bloody well ban religion, then there'd be no more boring Wanker Williams tormenting me daily. I would also make Kelly Parker shit herself in assembly in front of the whole school, and I would turn Roger Bostock's hair blonde and marry him and have lots of sex… I haven't actually had sex yet, but I'm pretty sure I'd like it because I once snogged my cousin's mate who was a year older than me and he put his hand inside my bra and it was great! (*Suddenly.*) You know what? Heather Pleby, right, she's always going on about sex like she's done it, but she hasn't and she can't anyway because she's too fat; she's even fatter than Kelly Parker if that's possible, and she thinks she's too good for H&M, but that's only because they haven't got her size – her voice just goes through me; it's high-pitched, nasty and bitchy –

HEATHER: You talkin' 'bout me?

FROM SCENE 2, PAGE 30…

KATIE: (*To audience.*) And then the pair of them march off like the bloody Gestapo to terrorise some other poor, unsuspecting kid. School is just full of weirdos like that; there's hardly anybody normal. Like Melanie Watson, who I do admit I kind of like after having been to her house and ate chips from a box and stuff, but right she and her Mum both smoke – *together…*

MUM: You got any fags, Mel?

MEL: Fuck off Mum, you fuckin' scrounger!

KATIE: And they go clubbing together… (*To audience.*) An' she's only bloody fourteen! (*Suddenly.*) So…where was I? Oh yeah, (*To DAD.*) so right Dad – I've got RE and maths and Wank…um, Mr Williams is like setting an exam next week; why I don't know, he must think it's funny or something, and so I've got to revise for it and then…

DAD: All right, all right, I don't want to know. I don't care how much homework you have; I still expect you to keep your room tidy.

FROM SCENE 2, PAGE 31…

KATIE: (*To audience.*) And like, do they seriously think I'd let either of them pop my cherry? The grubby, dirty little losers…and then there's Andy Blackwell who is really special…

ANDY: (*Mad smile.*) Hello Katie.

KATIE: (*To audience.*) Bless him.

ANDY: (*Mad smile.*) Hello.

KATIE: I don't know what's wrong with him, but something is, bless him – he's really short; but not as short as Jason, the wannabe gangsta, who reckons he's got a gun and is going out with someone in the year above…

JASON: (*Radical gesture.*) Radical innit?

KATIE: (*To herself.*) Whatever Jason! (*To audience.*) And then there's bloody Billy-Africa's-shit-Bradley who's always gets drunk and goes on about Ethiopia all the time…

BILLY: (*Drunk.*) You've no idea what those people suffer, no idea, man…

KATIE: (*To audience.*) And I'm like… (*To BILLY.*) Yes Billy, we do – it's terrible in Ethiopia and everybody's dying there or getting killed or being droughted on…but like move on! (*To audience.*) Lee Hammond's all right though – he's funny…

LEE: Hey, Katie guess who I saw last night?

KATIE: Dunno Lee – who?

LEE: Everybody I looked at!

KATIE: (*Laughs hysterically.*) And so we all danced together and Sam was like a bit pissed and suddenly decided to pluck up the courage to ask MJ for a dance and then she cried all night 'cause he wouldn't until we forced him too, and then she was all right until he told her that we'd forced him; then she cried all night again…

SAM: Why doesn't he like me? Am I like ugly or something?

KATIE: And Treena Sharples was pissed in the toilet all night trying to slash her wrists with a piece of wire while Heather Pleby banged on the door and slagged everyone off that came near. She scared poor Verity Edwards shitless…

FROM SCENE 3, PAGE 36…

KATIE: (*To audience.*) That is so unfair! It's like whatever I say, it's always Tidy your room, young lady! Bloody food fanatic, feeding me poor little Moroccan baa lambs.

LAMB: Baa, baa; don't eat me, Katie! I'm only three days old – I don't want to end up being sicked up in the toilet.

KATIE: I'm sorry lambykins, I really am, but what choice do I have? He's a mad food fanatic.

LAMB: Baa, baa! Why can't I hop and skip around the Moroccan hilltops with my brothers and sisters and be tucked up in the warm hay at night time by my sheepy mummy?

KATIE: Because you were destined to become a vital ingredient in a classic Mediterranean dish cooked by a mad old man with a passion to torment his obese daughter…sorry little furry white creature, I really am.

LAMB: Baa, baa! I hope he appreciates the fact that my pure innocent lamby blood has been spilled for his culinary obsession…

KATIE: (*Suddenly to audience.*) Hey, we had this lecture last week right about blood transfusion, and it just went on and bloody on and like everyone was just almost falling off their chairs because the man from the blood transfusion service was just droning on and on, and his voice was just like on one level like some boring robot, and come to think of it he did actually look like a vampire – his face was really white, like he was like the undead or something and he had this really grey matted hair that looked like he'd never washed it – ever, and he was just droning on and on about platelets and blood groups and OB fucking negative/ positive bloody rhesus bollocks, and Sam who hates anything to do with bodily functions is heaving away, and Oliver Bunting is kicking the chair in front to wake up twat face Billy-Africa's-shit-Bradley, who I swear was actually snoring, and then Dracula suddenly stopped speaking and switched off his bloody Power Point projection of some geeky old git of a nerdy business woman, grinning like a fucking gibbon while some nurse was jabbing a needle the size of a javelin in her arm like she was actually enjoying the experience. So we all started to rub our eyes and cough and fidget; and Oliver Bunting kicked Billy Bradley again even though he was plainly awake now, and then Mr Bloodsucker from the National Bloodsucker Vampire Service says...

VAMPIRE: I hope you all enjoyed the lecture and that it has inspired you when older to give blood.

KATIE: (*To audience.*) And Sam is still heaving away and I'm thinking Oh my God – she's gonna chuck up! And then Nosferatu says does anyone have any questions about donating? And of course it's like totally silent because who gives a flying fuck? And then Mr Wanker Williams speaks up...

WILLIAMS: Come on – a question for our guest, a question. Come on year ten –

KATIE: (*To audience.*) And he looks like he's just sucked a lemon; his face all twisted and sour, and I think *oh shut the fuck up, you wanker!* And then I think of a question and before I know it my hand's up and everyone's looking at me like *what the fuck is she doing?* But it's too late because Dracula spots me with his infra-red bat eyes and points at me smiling in a really creepy way...

VAMPIRE: Ah yes – the girl over there with the lovely blonde hair.

KATIE: *Lovely blonde hair* – pervy bloody paedophile! And Wanker Williams is glaring at me like Hitler and says...

WILLIAMS: Katie Weller, I hope you have some interesting point to share with our guest, I really do...

KATIE: (*To audience.*) And his eyes narrowed like he's sighting me up in a cross-hair...

WILLIAMS: ... Yes I really do, Katie Weller – for your sake I really do.

KATIE: (*To audience.*) And like I'm thinking: *shit, why did I bother, why did I bloody bother, because it's only going to end in disaster.* But it's too late and so I have no choice but to speak, so Dracula grins like some decaying zombie…

VAMPIRE: I'm sure Blonde Katie has an interesting point to share with us all, so –

KATIE: (*To audience.*) And everyone's looking, and so like there's no going back and I think it's okay actually because it's like a really like interesting point, so I say… 'Yes actually, I do have a question…'

VAMPIRE: And what is it Miss Blonde Katie Weller?

KATIE: (*To audience.*) Blonde Katie Weller! What is his problem? And I want to say: *why doesn't the paedophile police come and arrest him and hammer a stake through his vampire heart?* But instead I sigh a big weary sodding hell-why-did-I-bother-putting-my-hand-up kind of sigh and say… 'Well my question is can you donate fat'? (*To audience.*) And the vampire looks confused and gapes like the undead zombie he is and eventually he says…

VAMPIRE: *Fat?* What do you mean; *can you donate fat?*

KATIE: Can you donate fat? It's a simple enough question – can you donate fat? (*To audience.*) And Wanker Williams looks furious, like I'm taking the piss or something; but I'm not it's a perfectly honest question… 'Yeah because I mean there must be like loads of anorexic people who could do with some, and all those starving people in Africa, and if you wanna lose a few pounds it would be great if you could just walk into like a Fat Donation Centre and donate a few pounds, and like you'd be helping someone who needs it and shedding a bit of weight at the same time – so everybody wins!' (*To audience.*) And then I realise that everyone is looking at me and some of them are starting to laugh out loud; especially Kelly fat-face Parker, who would have done really well by my idea of donating fat (although it would have taken quite a few visits in her case), and I'm going red and Wanker Williams is going purple, and old Dracula truly looks like a creature of the night and is staring at me like he is damning my eternal soul forever, and says…

VAMPIRE: People who donate blood do so to save lives

KATIE: (*To audience.*) And instead of just shutting up, I'm like feeling really pissed off with the situation and the fact that everyone is laughing at me that I just carry on... 'Yeah, well fat donations could save lives too, couldn't it? And if I was like some flaky model hooked on drugs and heroin and stuff, yeah? And like there was like a fashion show where they wanted models who weren't all skinny and anorexic, well some podgy girl's fat might just save the day for her, right'? (*To audience.*) And now the whole hall is rocking and Sophie and Tori and all the rest of the girls are like wetting themselves, and Sophie sticks her thumb up like she thinks I'm taking the piss, so I feel you're on a roll, girl – the audience is yours! And so I stick my hands on my hips and go... 'Yeah, I think you've got it all wrong – forget blood, do fat'! (*To audience.*) And the hall is rocking, and like Oliver Bunting and his posse are whooping and shouting...

OLIVER: *Go on Katie!*

KATIE: (*To audience.*) And stuff like that, so I say again... 'Yeah – do fat'! (*To audience.*) And Wanker Williams shouts...

WILLIAMS: No Katie Weller – *do detention!*

KATIE: (*To audience.*) And then Sam threw up on my feet...well it was great while it lasted... (*Suddenly glum.*) Sophie's took me off her top ten on her My Space...

FROM SCENE 4, PAGE 42…

KATIE: (*To audience.*) And I couldn't believe that that fugly ho-bag slut would even dare to criticise my dress sense when she looked like King fucking Kong in her skinny leggings with a disgusting camel toe and muffin top cellulite dripping out, and her vomit looking sick-green coloured top that was so tight and low that she had pale white armpit flab, bingo wings and pushed-up man-boob cleavage like a great big crevice! But no, the fat tart really did have the audacity to say…

KELLY: Bit short… I thought you didn't like your legs.

FROM SCENE 4, PAGE 43…

KATIE: Tell me about it! (*To audience.*) So we chatted for a while and slagged off a few bitches and bullies, and I began to feel a bit better, and then Rachel came over too, and she was really nice as well…

RACHEL: Hello Katie, looking forward to your ballet show.

KATIE: You're coming to see it?

RACHEL: (*Shyly.*) A friend of mine's in it. I saw you last year too – you were fantastic.

KATIE: Don't know about that. Who's your friend?

RACHEL: Caroline, Caroline Bodenstein.

KATIE: Oh Caroline, yeah she's great.

RACHEL: We used to do classes together; but she's a lot better than me.

KATIE: Wow, you do ballet too!

RACHEL: At Miss Baker's, but like I'm only grade five.

KATIE: Grade five's good.

RACHEL: Not as good as you. She was great, Vez – you should have seen her.

KATIE: (*Proudly to audience.*) And then the rest of their posse came over and it was really nice, 'cause they were talking about me and about how good I was at ballet, and normally I'd have to keep it to myself, and I almost gave it up 'cause it's like so uncool and stuff; so it felt great to be able to talk about it and even brag a bit…but then Kelly and the others came round the corner and saw me talking to them like I was desperate, or something, and I could see they were laughing and I just choked up again and had to got to the toilets and just cry. So anyway I rang Dad to come and pick me up early, and he knew I was upset, and all the way home, he just kept on…

SCENE 5, PAGE 46...

KATIE: *Fine!* (*To audience.*) He came...he came to the show; I saw him in the audience, smiling like a fucking Cheshire fucking cat...with a girl. You could tell they were close, she kept nudging him and whispering in his ear; know what? I think he was just playing a game with me, the redheaded bastard! Just stringing me along for a joke, and then just rubbing my face in it with his bloody girlfriend! She was beautiful actually, really slim and a great figure and I bet she's really clever and all...bitch! (*Tearful.*) I really thought he liked me... I thought he fancied me and was going to ask me out. How could I have been so stupid! Why would someone like him fancy an ugly fat cow like me! I was with Caroline Bodenstein backstage, 'cause I had told her that Roger was coming and that he was really cool and handsome and intelligent and that he fancied me to pieces, so we peeped through the curtains...

CAROLINE: Can you see him?

KATIE: He's got the most amazing ginger hair; you can't miss him.

CAROLINE: (*Pointing.*) Is that him?

KATIE: Yeah, oh wow he came! *He really came!*

CAROLINE: Oh my God, Katie – *he's gorgeous!* You jammy sod!

KATIE: Hang on, who's that with him?

CAROLINE: That girl?

KATIE: Yeah.

CAROLINE: Don't you know her?

KATIE: Never seen her before in my life.

CAROLINE: Oh...well perhaps they're just friends.

KATIE: Yeah...probably. (*To audience.*) But I knew it for what it was. So I had to go out there and dance my little heart out for that son-of-a-bitch ginger cunt's warped sense of humour. On the way out, he even had the fucking gall to hang around, grinning and taking the piss...

FROM SCENE 6, PAGE 50…

KATIE: And I thought *what a nice girl!* And so we started hanging out and like they are just *nice girls*; they're not bitchy at all, well not *that* bitchy, 'cause you've got to bitch a bit, but they don't slag people off to their face and make them feel stupid like Sophie and Kelly and all. (*Suddenly*) Guess what – Melanie Foster is pregnant! I can't believe it! Actually I can; I think it was always on the cards with her, but you know she is like so sweet – she wants me to be a godmother; isn't that sweet? She really likes me you know. I went round her house again 'cause we did another detention, and for once her Mum wasn't in bed, but was actually in the kitchen and she cooked us something…

MUM: Hello me little darling, how are you today, been chundering again?

MEL: Nah, just feel a bit, y' know –

MUM: You ain't been smokin' have yer?

MEL: (*Irritated.*) No Mum.

MUM: Better not, either.

KATIE: (*To audience.*) And get this, her Mum actually seems quite pleased about it all…

MUM: What d' yer think of our little Melanie, eh? Gonna be a mummy!

KATIE: Yeah – it's great.

MUM: She could've got rid of it, like but she's decided to go ahead; I'm so proud of her.

MEL: What's for fuckin' dinner then Mum?

MUM: Grilled trout with a nice salad!

MEL: Aw Mum that's disgusting!

MUM: You have to eat properly now; you're eating for two, need yer vitamin C an' yer omega oils.

MEL: Aw Mum, can't I just have fuckin' pizza? I'm sick of this healthy eatin' shit.

MUM: I will not 'ave you fuckin' about with my grandchild's future thank you very much! Would you like some carrot juice, Katie?

KATIE: (*To audience.*) Said she could come back to my place one night and have some proper food. She won't tell me who the dad is though; probably some bloke from one those clubs she goes to…

MEL: All I'm saying is he's got really blue eyes, very tall and fit and blonde hair like me.

KATIE: (*To audience.*) She dyes it! (*Smiles.*) Right are you ready for this? I have actually got a boyfriend – I have!

THANKS

I would like to thank the following people for their help and inspiration in this project: my daughter, Lucy Jones and her friends; especially Ella Davison, my director, Amy Bonsall, my designer Maira Vazeou, Ken Chistiansen (who made it all happen), Jenny Fellows and Amy Hodge from Operating Theatre Company, my agent Georgina Ruffhead from David Higham Associates, Theresa Heskins, Sarah Jones, Saskia Sutton, Ed Bury and finally Stephen Watson and Daisy Bowie-Sell from Oberon books.